S. ANTONINI

Agile Scrum Culture

Discover How Scrum Fosters Deep Connections, Streamlines Communication, and Creates a Tight-Knit, High-Energy Organization

Copyright © 2024 by S. Antonini

All rights reserved. No part of this publication may be reproduced, stored or transmitted in any form or by any means, electronic, mechanical, photocopying, recording, scanning, or otherwise without written permission from the publisher. It is illegal to copy this book, post it to a website, or distribute it by any other means without permission.

S. Antonini asserts the moral right to be identified as the author of this work.

S. Antonini has no responsibility for the persistence or accuracy of URLs for external or third-party Internet Websites referred to in this publication and does not guarantee that any content on such Websites is, or will remain, accurate or appropriate.

Designations used by companies to distinguish their products are often claimed as trademarks. All brand names and product names used in this book and on its cover are trade names, service marks, trademarks and registered trademarks of their respective owners. The publishers and the book are not associated with any product or vendor mentioned in this book. None of the companies referenced within the book have endorsed the book.

First edition

This book was professionally typeset on Reedsy.
Find out more at reedsy.com

Contents

Introduction	1
1 The Foundations of Agile Scrum	3
Origins of Agile and Scrum	3
The Agile Manifesto: A Declaration of Interdependence	5
The Cast of Characters: The Heroes of Scrum	7
2 Building Deep Connections	10
Fostering Collaboration	10
Enhancing Communication	12
Building Trust & Respect	14
3 Creating a High-Energy Work Environment	17
Energizing Your Team	17
Motivational Practices	19
Managing Energy Levels	20
4 Continuous Improvement and Innovation	23
Kaizen and Agile	23
Innovation Practices	25
Feedback and Adaptation	27
5 The Agile Scrum Revolution	29
6 Reference List	31

Introduction

Picture a company so disorganized that they'd have taken home the gold every year if clutter were an Olympic sport. Their project timelines were more tangled than a bowl of spaghetti, and the team spirit was as damp as socks after a puddle-jumping contest. Then, Agile Scrum entered the scene like a referee ready to clean up a particularly unruly game.

This was the everyday reality at Chaos Inc., an ambitious startup where the business plan looked more like a treasure map, and every meeting was an endurance test that could rival a marathon. Productivity was as elusive as a polite political debate, existing more in theory than practice. But that all changed when they embraced Agile Scrum. With an Agile Scrum culture, their projects became neatly organized, meeting deadlines with accuracy. Chaos Inc. morphed from a band of misfit procrastinators into a squadron of sprint champions, proving that even the messiest of teams could find their rhythm and not just meet their goals but dance through them.

This book isn't just about another business strategy but a revolution in working together. Agile Scrum isn't merely a methodology—it's a lifeline to companies drowning in the details. At the heart of Agile Scrum is the power to enhance communication, streamline processes, and energize organizations. It transforms groups of individuals into close-knit teams that not only meet deadlines but also have a blast doing it and create a powerful organization.

As we flip the pages of this book, we'll dig deeper into understanding Agile and Scrum and the importance of a strong Culture.

First, we'll demystify Agile and Scrum. What are they? Where did they come from? And how did they become the darlings of software development and beyond? We'll break it down with straightforward explanations and sprinkle in thought-provoking transformation scenarios. Think of it as a journey back to the basics with a twist of fun.

Next, we dive deep into the cultural revolution that Agile Scrum can ignite. It's not just about getting things done faster; it's about fostering a workplace where people genuinely enjoy their work. We'll explore how a positive culture can accelerate productivity and make every day feel like a win.

By the end of this book, you won't just understand Agile Scrum; you'll believe in its power to transform the fabric of an organization's culture. Prepare to laugh, learn, and leap into a new way of working where business meets pleasure and teams become families. Welcome to the culture of Agile Scrum—where work is serious fun, and every sprint is a step toward greatness.

1

The Foundations of Agile Scrum

Origins of Agile and Scrum

Did you know? Projects managed under Agile methodologies have a success rate of 64%, compared to just 49% for projects tackled with traditional methods. That's right; Agile projects are more likely to succeed than a slice of pizza at a high school party is to disappear!

History and Evolution

Once upon a time, in the not-so-distant 1990s, the software development world was as slow-moving as a dial-up internet connection. Projects were mammoth, and their technology was about as cutting-edge as a floppy disk by the time they were done. That's when a group of 17 software developers went on a legendary ski trip, not just to schuss and shred but to change the world of software development forever.

They created the Agile Manifesto, a revolutionary document that favored "individuals and interactions over processes and tools" and "responding to change over following a plan." Agile Scrum sprang from this seed, designed to tackle projects like a series of quick sprints instead of a single marathon. This approach wasn't just a change in speed; it was like swapping out an old, creaky bicycle for a turbocharged motorcycle.

Core Principles and Values

Agile Scrum is built on pillars that could double as life mottos if you're exceptionally organized. The core principles include:

- **individuals and interactions** *over processes,*
- **working software** *over comprehensive documentation,*
- **customer collaboration** *over contract negotiation,*
- **responding to change** *over following a plan*

It's like saying, "Hey, let's actually talk to each other, get stuff done, keep our clients happy, and ride the waves of change like pro surfers!"

The values? They're all about *commitment, courage, focus, openness, and respect.* Imagine a workplace where these aren't just plaque-worthy words but the real deal. Everyone's wearing superhero capes, but instead of an "S" for Superman, there's a "C" for Commitment!

Key Differences from Traditional Methods

Traditional project management could be like planning a wedding with a five-year engagement. Everything is mapped out, from the napkin colors to the exact timing of the toasts. Agile Scrum, on the other hand, is more like a pop-up wedding. It's quick, adaptable, and ready for surprises. It focuses on delivering functional chunks of work, iterating rapidly, and adapting to change.

Traditional methods often silo information and bog down projects with heavy documentation, while Agile Scrum thrives on collaboration and quick, effective communication—kind of like swapping out telegrams for instant messaging.

* * *

The Agile Manifesto: A Declaration of Interdependence

The Agile Manifesto is comparable to a historic declaration in the software development world. Unlike its political counterparts' heavy, solemn tones, this declaration is about lightening up—both the workload and the mood!

The Four Values

At its core, the Agile Manifesto champions four groundbreaking values that could easily be mistaken for relationship advice:

1. **Individuals and Interactions Over Processes and Tools:** This value champions people over paperwork. It's like choosing to actually talk to your roommate instead of leaving passive-aggressive notes on the fridge about laundry etiquette.
2. **Working Software Over Comprehensive Documentation:** Why write a novel about software when you could just show a working demo? It's the equivalent of choosing a cake tasting over reading a cookbook.
3. **Customer Collaboration Over Contract Negotiation:** Imagine planning a party with your friends by asking what they'd enjoy instead of just giving them an itinerary. This value is all about keeping the doors open and the conversation flowing.
4. **Responding to Change Over Following a Plan:** This is like preferring improvisational dance moves over a rigid ballet routine. It's about being flexible and ready to pivot rather than stubbornly sticking to the plan when the music changes.

The Twelve Principles of Software Development

> # 12 Principles of Agile Software Development
> 1. Satisfy the customer through early and continuous delivery.
> 2. Welcome changing requirements, even late in development.
> 3. Deliver working software frequently
> 4. Business people and developers work together daily
> 5. Build projects around motivated individuals.
> 6. Convey information via face-to-face conversation.
> 7. Working software is the primary measure of progress.
> 8. Maintain a constant pace indefinitely.
> 9. Give continuous attention to technical excellence
> 10. Simplify: maximizing the amount of work not done
> 11. Teams self-organize.
> 12. Teams retrospect and tune behavior

Figure 1

According to Jeffries (2009), the principles of agile software development emphasize continuous improvement and flexible responses to change. (see Fig. 1) These principles are like the secret sauce that makes the Agile values work. They range from satisfying the customer through early and continuous delivery to maintaining a constant pace indefinitely. Other highlights include welcoming changing requirements, building projects around motivated individuals, and having face-to-face conversations, which are the high-octane fuel for successful collaboration.

These values and principles aren't just operational guidelines but catalysts for cultural transformation. They foster environments where innovation is expected, communication is critical, and flexibility is encouraged and celebrated. It's a culture where the workspace turns from a grid of cubicles into a dynamic playground where creativity and productivity play nicely together.

Agile Scrum in Modern Organizations

Modern organizations have enthusiastically embraced Agile. Companies across industries find that applying these values and principles improves software development and revolutionizes the entire business process and culture.

Imagine marketing teams iterating campaign strategies like software sprints, HR departments engaging in continuous feedback loops, and executives prioritizing people over spreadsheets. It's like turning the whole company into a jazz band where everyone improvises yet somehow ends up in perfect harmony.

By embedding the Agile Manifesto into their core, organizations don't just do Agile; they become Agile. They transform into places where work feels less like work and more like a part of a meaningful, responsive community. This shift isn't just beneficial—it's revolutionary, paving the way for businesses that are not only successful but also genuinely joyful places to work.

* * *

The Cast of Characters: The Heroes of Scrum

Every epic tale has heroes whose roles are pivotal to the story line. In the world of Agile Scrum, we don't just have heroes; we have champions of efficiency, guardians of the backlog, and wizards of code. Let's meet the cast of Scrum, shall we?

The Scrum Master

First up, the Scrum Master – not to be mistaken for a Jedi Master, although both share an affinity for guiding others and maintaining peace. Think of the Scrum Master as the ultimate facilitator, who's less about wielding power and more about empowering, ensuring everything runs smoothly, and handling impediments like a skilled juggler.

The Scrum Master is the team's cheerleader, coach, and sometimes therapist. Their job is to keep everyone on the Agile path, mediate conflicts, and ensure that the Scrum practices are followed.

The Product Owner

Enter the Product Owner: part visionary, part pragmatist. The Product Owner is the voice of the customer within the team and is responsible for defining the product's vision and prioritizing the work or 'backlog' based on business value.

Imagine them as a master curator at a museum, deciding which art pieces (or features) make it to the exhibit for public admiration. They're the bridge between the business side and the technical team, ensuring every sprint is a step towards a delivered masterpiece.

The Development Team

And then we have the Development Team – the wizards behind the curtain, the builders of the digital world. In Scrum, this isn't just any team; it's a self-organizing ensemble of skilled professionals who code, test, and design. The Development Team works in sprints, short, consistent cycles, to turn the Product Owner's vision into a tangible product. They're the heart of the operation, pumping out features and fixes with precision.

These roles are the pillars Scrum stands on, but they're more than just job descriptions. They embody a shift in workplace dynamics and culture. You might find strict hierarchies and siloed departments in a traditional setting, but Scrum flips this on its head. It champions collaboration, cross-functionality, and a flat structure where leadership is about facilitation, not dictation.

The interaction between these roles fosters an environment of open communication, mutual respect, and collective accountability. Each role supports and enhances the others, creating a tight-knit tribe that can face any challenge with agility and grace.

By integrating these roles, organizations set the stage for a culture that values flexibility, adapts quickly to change, and embraces challenges with a can-do attitude. This culture produces better products and happier people, turning the daily grind into an opportunity to innovate and excite. This is the essence of Agile Scrum culture: a workplace where everyone is engaged, empowered, and enthusiastically part of something great.

This chapter isn't just a history lesson; it's a blueprint for transformation. By championing principles like embracing change and prioritizing human interaction over rigid processes, they set the stage for a profound cultural shift within organizations. This is the magic of Agile Scrum: turning the mundane into the extraordinary, one sprint at a time.

2

Building Deep Connections

Fostering Collaboration

Once lived a team so disjointed that even the coffee machine gave up trying to bring them together for a morning chat. In this maze of missed messages and siloed workers, the team members were more familiar with the backs of each other's heads than their morning faces. That was until Agile Scrum came into their lives, turning their tower of babble into a close-knit powerhouse of productivity and camaraderie.

In the world of Scrum, our foundation is built on teamwork, and it's not just about business but also about getting a bit personal: the Daily Stand-up, Collaborative Planning Sessions, and the Retrospective—because who we are and what we contribute deserves more than just a nod; it deserves a whole meeting!

Daily Stand-ups

Daily stand-ups transformed from dreaded monologues into something resembling a family breakfast table. Each morning, the team gathered for a quick 15-minute sync, sharing their progress, plans, and any roadblocks. It wasn't just about keeping the work on track; it was about turning strangers into teammates who actually *knew* each other beyond their email addresses.

Bob from accounting, previously known only by his meticulous spreadsheets, shares his weekend hiking adventures. Suddenly, Bob isn't just a spreadsheet guru but a respected mountain climber every Monday morning.

These stand-ups aren't just about updates but about weaving personal connections that strengthen professional ones.

Collaborative Planning Sessions

Next, we have collaborative planning sessions, which are like group brainstorming sessions on steroids. Everyone has a voice here, and ideas fly around like popcorn at a movie premiere. These sessions were crucial for planning the next sprint and building a road map in which everyone felt invested.

In one memorable session, the team tackled a particularly thorny problem that had been a project roadblock for weeks. With everyone contributing—from the quietest coder to the most outspoken marketer—the solution came from an unexpected source: the intern, who turned out to have a knack for out-of-the-box thinking. It was a lightbulb moment that taught the team the value of every voice, setting the stage for future innovations.

Retrospectives

Retrospectives are the cherry on top of the collaboration cake. Held at the end of each sprint, these are not your typical post-mortem meetings where the air is thick with the dread of blame. Instead, they were constructive, forward-looking, and often peppered with laughter over past snafus-turned-learning experiences.

One retrospective involved a 'lessons learned' segment that quickly devolved into a hilarious recounting of a miscommunication that led to programming a feature incorrectly. Instead of finger-pointing, there was chuckling and a unanimous decision to implement clearer communication channels. The team improved their work and bonds through these retrospectives as they collectively celebrated victories and learned from defeats.

Streamlined communication is what holds everything together. It turns potential misunderstandings into moments of clarity and conflict into collaboration. Without it, you're just a group working on the same project but not working *together*. These are more than mere tools; they are rituals that cultivate a sense of belonging and a shared mission. These practices ensure that everyone remains included and informed, transforming the workplace from simply a place to work into a space where we can all thrive together.

* * *

Enhancing Communication

Once upon a time, a team was so siloed that if you shouted into one department, the echo wouldn't reach the next until the following week. But then, Agile Scrum came in, armed with tools not just to break down walls but to transform them into windows of transparency and doorways of dialogue.

Open Communication Channels

Open communication channels in Scrum are like the gossip columns of the corporate world—only productive and less scandalous. Before Scrum, our team's idea of "open communication" was sending emails that CC'd half the company. With Scrum, we switched to daily stand-ups where everyone could spill the beans on their latest tasks and tackle issues more dynamically. It was less about airing dirty laundry and more about sharing freshly laundered ideas.

Jenny from design finally tells Tom from software about her vision in real-time, not via a trail of outdated emails. The result? Fewer misinterpretations, faster clarifications, and camaraderie.

Feedback Loops

Feedback loops in Scrum are like boomerangs; you send something out, and it comes right back with insights you didn't even know you needed. In the pre-Scrum days, feedback was often as timely as a holiday card arriving in January. However, with Scrum, feedback loops are built into every sprint, ensuring no one is ever out of the loop.

During retrospectives, everyone throws their two cents into the pot. Imagine the scene: After a sprint, the team gathers, and instead of pointing fingers, they pass around the "talking stick" of constructive criticism.

Transparency in Processes

Transparency in Scrum isn't just about clear windows; it's about glass doors, glass floors—heck, even glass ceilings. Everything about the work is visible to everyone, from timelines to to-dos. This crystal-clear visibility ensures that everyone knows what everyone else is up to, which is about as secretive as a reality TV show but significantly more productive.

This level of openness means that when someone spots a snag, the whole team can rally to untangle it quicker than you can say, "Scrum savior." It's like turning on the lights at a surprise party; everyone knows what's happening and can jump right into the celebration—or problem-solving, in this case.

This initiative that Scrum encourages is the honey that keeps everything sweet. It's not just about talking more; it's about talking better. Open channels, constant feedback, and transparent processes ensure that information flows. This communicative culture doesn't just make projects run smoother; it turns colleagues into collaborators, skeptics into supporters, and groups into tightly-knit teams. It's the secret sauce that spices up the workspace, ensuring every day is an opportunity to connect, create, and conquer challenges together.

Through open channels, feedback, and transparency practices, disconnected individuals become a high-energy, synergistic team capable of tackling complex solutions with a smile. It's not just about building products; it's about building relationships. In Agile Scrum, every message, meeting, and mishap is a chance to strengthen these bonds, turning everyday interactions into the threads that weave the fabric of a dynamic, thriving organization.

* * *

Building Trust & Respect

Meet the Widgets Inc. team, a group once so riddled with mistrust that even their smartphones had trust issues. Emails were as guarded as royal secrets, and meetings felt like minor cold wars. But thanks to Scrum, they transformed into a tightly knit team that could collectively make a sweater for an elephant without dropping a stitch!

Trust-Building Exercises

In the revamped Widgets Inc., trust-building exercises became as routine as daily morning stretches. Instead of traditional team-building traps like trust falls (which, let's be honest, were never a good idea after that incident with Bob and the jelly doughnut), they adopted Scrum rituals tailored to build trust incrementally. For instance, team members took turns leading the session during sprint planning, showcasing their strengths and vulnerabilities.

Imagine a "Professional Truth or Dare" game in which each member shares one professional strength and one weakness. This would illuminate diverse skill sets and highlight areas where they could depend on each other, turning potential weaknesses into team-wide assets.

Encouraging Mutual Respect

Mutual respect in this newly formed agile team meant seeing more than just job titles; it was about acknowledging each member's contributions as essential cogs in the great innovation machine. Scrum's emphasis on cross-functionality—where developers, designers, and testers collaborate closely—meant that no one could claim the spotlight alone.

To foster this environment, Widgets Inc. introduced "Appreciation Sprints," where team members highlighted each other's contributions at the end of each sprint. It wasn't just about applauding the big wins but also the tiny assists that kept the project rolling, like the quiet coder who optimized a snarly bit of code or the designer who stayed late tweaking a UI to perfection.

Conflict Resolution Strategies

Conflict was inevitable, but Scrum gave them the tools to handle disagreements with more finesse than a diplomat at a peace talk. Retrospectives turned into safe arenas where issues were raised and resolved constructively. The team adopted a "conflict is fuel" approach, using disagreements as a springboard for innovation rather than a sinkhole for morale.

They employed techniques like "Issue Mapping," where conflicts were broken down into components and tackled individually. This often revealed that the root of a heated argument was just a miscommunication or a mismatch in priorities.

In this culture, trust wasn't just a nice to have; it was the foundation of their collective strength. It allowed them to tackle challenges with a united front, transforming potential obstacles into stepping stones toward their shared goals. As the team's trust grew, so did their success, proving that when communication flows clearly, and respect is mutual, there's no limit to what a well-aligned team can achieve.

Through Scrum, Widgets Inc. improved its productivity; it built a fortress of trust and respect, where each team member wasn't just a worker but a valued player in a grand, collaborative game. In this environment, building deep connections wasn't just a goal—it was the inevitable outcome of its daily practices.

This chapter discusses how Agile Scrum revolutionizes project management and masterfully weaves a web of more profound, meaningful relationships within teams. Agile Scrum transforms the daily grind into a blend of personalities, ideas, and shared goals, setting the stage for a cultural shift where work becomes synonymous with connection and creativity.

3

Creating a High-Energy Work Environment

Energizing Your Team

Energy is the currency of high-performing teams. In the bustling market of today's work environments, this currency buys more than just productivity—it powers passion, drives innovation, and fuels every sprint to success. So, let's make it rain!

Setting Exciting Goals

Setting goals in an Agile Scrum environment is like being a kid with a map in an amusement park. Every map point is thrilling, and every completed game brings you one step closer to winning that giant stuffed teddy bear. In Scrum, these goals aren't just milestones—they're missions. Each sprint goal is crafted to achieve something on paper and challenge the team, spark their enthusiasm, and align with their passions.

Imagine starting each sprint by asking, "What awesome feat will we accomplish this time?" This approach turns routine project objectives into quests that are as engaging as a season finale cliffhanger—everyone's on the edge of their seats, eager to see what happens next.

Celebrating Small Wins

In a high-energy Scrum culture, celebrating small wins is a constant thought. It's about recognizing and cheering every little success along the way, just like giving a high five on every excellent play in a game. Whether it's perfecting a line of code or nailing a client presentation, each win is a sparkler at the team's victory party.

At the end of each sprint, it's a mini-Oscar night, where achievements are highlighted and celebrated. This boosts morale and reinforces the team's drive to push forward. It turns the daily grind into a sequence of victories, keeping the energy high and the team motivated.

Encouraging Creativity and Innovation

Encouraging creativity and innovation in a team is like tossing interesting ingredients into a blender and seeing what exciting new smoothie comes out. Agile Scrum environments provide the safety net of iterative processes, which means team members can throw in their wildest ideas without fear of messing up the whole project. It's about fostering a 'test and learn' mentality where every creative risk has the potential to lead to groundbreaking innovations.

Scrum teams are encouraged to brainstorm, prototype, and test as if their workspace were a lab for mad scientists—only much less dangerous and with a lot more collaboration. This vibe is not just invigorating; it's contagious, spreading creativity throughout the organization.

* * *

Motivational Practices

"In the realm of high-performing teams, enthusiasm isn't just a perk—it's the main course!"

Recognition & Rewards: More Than Just a Pat on the Back

At the heart of every high-energy workplace is a culture that knows a simple "thank you" might make someone's day, but a "thank you with a cherry on top" can make their month. Recognition in Agile Scrum teams isn't just about giving a shoutout during a meeting; it's about creating moments that make team members feel like rock stars on a world tour.

Imagine a company where each sprint's standout performer gets the "Golden Keyboard" award, complete with a mini-ceremony. It's fun and flashy, turning everyday accomplishments into headline news. This kind of recognition fuels a lively, vibrant workplace atmosphere, making the daily grind feel more like a daily giggle.

Continuous Learning Opportunities: Keeping the Brain Juicy

Much like a sponge, a brain works best when it's wet—with knowledge. Continuous learning opportunities in these environments are the juice that keeps the brain spongy and the ideas flowing. It's about fostering an atmosphere where learning is as expected as logging into your computer in the morning.

Take, for instance, a company that turns one lunch hour weekly into "Lunch and Learn" sessions, where team members share knowledge over pizza. It's casual and tasty, and it turns a regular lunch break into a feast of insights. Who knew learning could be as delightful as devouring your favorite slice?

Providing a Supportive Environment: It's Like Family, But Better

Creating a supportive environment means building a workplace that is more like your favorite family reunion—minus the awkward conversations. It's where everyone feels safe to speak their mind, challenge the status quo, and maybe even break things (metaphorically, mostly).

Imagine a company where "Fail Fridays" are a day dedicated to sharing what didn't work and exploring why without judgment or repercussions. It turns the fear of failure on its head, making it as welcome as an old friend, laughing together at what went wrong and learning for the next round.

***

Managing Energy Levels

"In the quest for high performance, remember that even superheroes need to take their capes off to wash them occasionally!"

Avoiding Burnout: Not Just for Candles

In the electric buzz of Agile environments, it's crucial to remember that human energy isn't infinite—unlike the number of emails one can get in an hour. Avoiding burnout isn't just about preventing exhaustion; it's about making sustainability the star of the show.

Take, for instance, the story of a team at WebCrafters Inc. Initially, they prided themselves on all-night coding sessions and caffeine-fueled deadlines. However, they soon realized that burnout was creeping in, turning their office vibe from "Let's do this!" to "Let's get this over with." They shifted gears by instituting mandatory "Log Off and Live" times, where the office lights literally dimmed at 6 PM, encouraging everyone to recharge their batteries—figuratively and literally. The result? A team that came back each morning with more spark and fewer yawns.

Balancing Workloads: Juggling, Scrum Style

Balancing workloads isn't about filling everyone's plate equally but ensuring nobody's plate resembles a rogue Thanksgiving dinner. It's crucial for maintaining an energized team—too little work and people get bored; too much and they get overwhelmed.

Scrum makes this easier with its transparent task management. At CloudConnect Solutions, they adopted a "Task Tally" approach, where team members could see their workload and their teammates. This visibility allowed them to pitch in and help balance the load, turning individual stress puddles into a well-managed workflow. It's like a potluck dinner; everyone brings something to the table, ensuring no one is stuck in the kitchen all night.

Promoting Work-Life Balance: Not Just a Buzzword

Work-life balance in an Agile Scrum culture is about understanding that employees have lives outside their tasks—shocking, right? It's about respecting personal and professional time and ensuring that the work environment promotes health and happiness.

Imagine a company like FunTech, where "Flexible Fridays" have been introduced, allowing team members to choose their working hours or work remotely. This flexibility acknowledges that life isn't just about work, and rest isn't just about sleep—it's about having the time to enjoy hobbies and family and occasionally binge-watching a series without feeling guilty. This policy didn't just improve morale; it turned weekends into a time of genuine relaxation and disconnection, so by Monday, everyone was more energized and engaged.

This provides a different look at how the Agile Scrum framework can transform a workplace into a veritable power plant of positivity and energy.

It emphasizes the importance of fostering a culture that encourages creativity and innovation and makes it a daily routine. It highlights how a positive culture isn't just excellent; it's essential for sustaining the high energy necessary for high performance. Energy levels soar in an environment where team members feel valued, recognized, and supported. This isn't the kind of energy you get from a sugar rush, which crashes as quickly as it spikes; it's more like a steady current that powers through each day.

Celebrations, creativity, and motivational practices become the fuel that keeps the engine running smoothly. This energetic atmosphere ensures that the daily grind is less about grinding down and more about gearing up for exciting challenges. It's a place where burnout is as rare as a dull moment, and maintaining high energy is as crucial as keeping the coffee pot full—essential for success and a whole lot of fun to create a working culture that fuels itself.

4

Continuous Improvement and Innovation

Kaizen and Agile

"Meet Innovatech Solutions, a company that sees innovation not just as a strategy but as their daily bread—always fresh and endlessly nourishing!"

The Concept of Continuous Improvement

Continuous improvement, or Kaizen, is a philosophy that, much like your favorite sitcom, always stays young. It's about the ongoing effort to improve products, services, or processes. In an Agile Scrum environment, this is not just a concept; it's a daily practice.

Innovatech Solutions, a mid-sized software development firm, embraced this philosophy wholeheartedly. They began viewing each project as a task to be completed and an opportunity to learn and enhance. Their motto? "There's always room for improvement, and yes, that includes the coffee machine!"

Applying Kaizen in Agile

In Agile, Kaizen translates into constant, incremental changes. It's about iterating, not just to fix things but to find better ways of doing them. Innovatech introduced a "Kaizen Sprint," whose sole focus was identifying workflow and process improvements. These sprints involved everyone from the CEO to the interns, turning the whole company into a dynamic think tank.

Every two weeks, the team gathered to review their processes, guided by feedback loops from their Agile practices. They asked questions like, "How can we code faster without sacrificing quality?" or "Is there a way to make our daily standups even more energizing?" Every session was a mix of severe brainstorming and lighthearted banter, proving that improvement can be fun, especially with the right amount of snacks.

Real-World Application

The impact of integrating Kaizen into Agile at Innovatech was profound. For instance, by refining their code review process, they reduced bug rates by 25% within a few months. Another practical outcome was enhancing their client feedback system, significantly improving customer satisfaction and retention.

Their story became a case study featured on several Agile community websites, such as ScrumAlliance.org and AgileAlliance.org, where they shared their journey and the specific tactics they employed. These platforms helped spread the word, inspiring other companies to adopt similar practices and creating a ripple effect in the Agile community.

The journey of Innovatech Solutions with Kaizen and Agile is more than just a story of business improvement. It's a testament to the power of treating every day as an opportunity to improve. Watch for these shifts to see if your team is embracing Kaizen and Agile;

- **Continuous Improvement is a Mindset, not an Action:** Just like your muscles, remember your gym routine, and your team can learn to look for ways to improve continually.

- **Kaizen in Agile is About Everyone:** From interns to executives, improvement is everyone's business. Think of it as a party where everyone's invited, and the party favor is a better way of working.

- **Sharing Real-World Applications Make a Difference:** Practical changes, inspired by everyday challenges and successes, lead to measurable improvements and can inspire an industry-wide evolution.

Innovatech's embrace of Kaizen within Agile wasn't just about keeping up; it was about leading the way and ensuring that every step forward was a step toward better, wiser, and more enjoyable working methods. Remember, in the world of Agile, improvement is not just a goal; it's part of the journey—so why not make it a fun ride?

***

Innovation Practices

"Dive into the story of CodeCrafters, a company that spins innovation out of their Agile loom like a tailor crafting a bespoke suit—perfectly fitted to each challenge!"

Hackathons and Innovation Sprints

At CodeCrafters, the traditional hackathon isn't just an event; it's a festival of creativity. These are not your average coffee-fueled coding marathons but vibrant innovation sprints, where teams rally for 24 to 48 hours to turn wild ideas into working prototypes. They've been known to produce everything from a new app feature that customers love to an internal tool that makes life easier for the sales team.

Imagine a carnival atmosphere where you have APIs and brainstorming sessions instead of rides and cotton candy. These hackathons have become a core part of their culture, celebrated with as much excitement as any holiday, with prizes for ideas ranging from the most technically impressive to the quirkiest.

Encouraging Experimentation

CodeCrafters lives by the motto, "If you're not trying something new, you're doing something old." Encouraging experimentation means that every team member—from interns to the CEO—is empowered to suggest and spearhead trials of new technologies and methodologies. This could be anything from testing a new programming language to adopting a radical new project management tool.

The company fosters an environment where the phrase "That's how we've always done it" is less welcome than a software bug at launch. This open-minded approach ensures that innovation isn't just an occasional spark but a continuous flame.

Learning from Failures

If CodeCrafters had a dollar for every failed experiment, they'd be funding their own space program. But here, failures aren't setbacks; they're stepping stones. Post-failure analyses are as standard as code reviews, and each misstep is dissected not for blame but for lessons.

They celebrate "Flop Fridays," a weekly session where teams share what didn't work and why. These aren't sad confessions but rather vibrant discussions that often end with laughter and, more importantly, learning.

Through Hackathons and innovation sprints, experimentation, and learning from failures, CodeCrafters doesn't just innovate; they create a vibrant tapestry of trial, error, and success that keeps the entire organization moving forward. This approach to continuous improvement and innovation ensures that the wheel of progress is always turning and, more importantly, everyone has a hand spinning it.

CONTINUOUS IMPROVEMENT AND INNOVATION

* * *

Feedback and Adaptation

"Let's zoom into GlobeTech, a Fortune 500 titan that treats Agile like its digital fountain of youth, continuously rejuvenating its strategies and products with youthful energy!"

Regular Feedback Loops

At GlobeTech, feedback isn't a once-a-year performance review horror show; it's as routine as their morning coffee—integral, energizing, and a little addictive. They've perfected the art of regular feedback loops where each team, from software developers to marketing gurus, engages in bi-weekly retrospectives to dissect what worked, what didn't, and how they can improve.

Picture this: their offices buzzing with lively discussions as diverse teams huddle around whiteboards decorated with colorful Post-it notes, each representing an idea, a critique, or a kudos. It's a bit like a brainstorming art gallery where every piece of feedback helps paint a broader picture of progress.

Adapting to Changes

Change at GlobeTech isn't just expected; it's embraced with the enthusiasm of a kid in a candy store. Agile Scrum powers their adaptability, enabling them to pivot faster. When a new market trend emerges, or a project veers off course, their Scrum rituals (like sprint planning and daily stand-ups) provide the structure to assess and adjust their course quickly.

This handy approach is crucial in today's fast-paced market. It's not uncommon to see a product team take a new customer insight from a feedback session and alter their development path by the next sprint. This agility ensures that GlobeTech stays ahead of the curve—or rather, invents new curves for others to follow.

Scaling Innovations

Once GlobeTech identifies a winning idea, scaling it isn't just a matter of pushing a button; it's an art form. First, they utilize the Scrum framework to test innovations on a small scale. Once validated, they use insights from their Agile processes to scale these innovations efficiently across different markets and teams.

The secret sauce? Their cross-functional squads operate like mini-startups, empowered to make decisions and scale successes without the red tape typically found in a corporate environment. This method speeds up innovation and consistently aligns with real-world feedback and needs.

At GlobeTech, and any organization wielding Agile with such finesse, the continuous improvement and innovation culture isn't just about keeping up. It's about leading, transforming, and sometimes having fun while at it. Remember, in the race for innovation, it's not just the speed but the agility to turn corners that wins the race.

Embracing Kaizen and Agile is like participating in an ongoing marathon where surprises await at every turn. This drives home the message that in Agile environments, improvement and innovation are not just about maintaining productivity; they're about supercharging and enjoying the journey. It's a dynamic, exhilarating approach to work where progress is as much about boosting spirits as it is about increasing efficiency.

5

The Agile Scrum Revolution

Agile Scrum is more than a methodology; it's a cultural revolution. At its core are principles and values that prioritize individuals, interactions, and adaptability over rigid processes. It fosters an environment where communication flows freely, trust is built, and respect is mutual. In this environment, teams thrive because they meet deadlines and enjoy the journey together.

Key Takeaways:

- Agile Scrum emerged from the need for flexibility and rapid iteration. It provides a practical and adaptable framework by embracing commitment, courage, focus, openness, and respect.
- Agile Scrum transforms teams from disjointed groups into close-knit units through daily standups, collaborative planning sessions, and retrospectives. These practices keep projects on track and build personal connections that strengthen professional relationships.
- Open communication channels, feedback loops, and transparency are the bedrock of Agile Scrum. They ensure that every team member is informed, included, and engaged, turning potential misunderstandings into opportunities for clarity and collaboration.
- Setting exciting goals, celebrating small wins, and encouraging creativity

and innovation keep the team's energy high. Recognition and rewards, continuous learning opportunities, and a supportive environment prevent burnout and ensure sustainable high performance.
- Integrating Kaizen with Agile principles fosters a culture of continuous improvement and innovation, enabling organizations to adapt quickly, enhance processes, and maintain high energy and morale.

As you reflect on these insights and apply them to your own organization, remember that Agile Scrum is not a one-size-fits-all solution but a flexible framework that can be tailored to your team's unique needs. It's about creating a workplace where everyone feels empowered, valued, and excited to contribute.

Implementing Agile Scrum requires continuous learning, adaptation, and a commitment to fostering a positive culture. The rewards are well worth the effort—greater productivity, higher morale, and a work environment where everyone looks forward to coming to work each day.

Agile Scrum emerges not just as a management tool but as a philosophy for life within the professional sphere. It champions an environment where every day is an opportunity to innovate, each task is a doorway to an adventure, and every team member is a crucial player in the game of progress and fuels creating tight-knit, high-energy organizations.

As we embrace it, let's carry forward the spirit of continuous improvement, deep connection, high energy, and relentless innovation. Let's not just do work—celebrate, live, and elevate it to an art form.

The Agile Scrum Culture isn't just a way to manage projects or work; it's a way to enrich lives, making every moment at work an opportunity to learn, grow, and enjoy. Here's to making every day more like a joyride on the high-speed train of professional fulfillment!

If you found this book helpful, I'd appreciate it if you left a favorable review on Amazon!

6

Reference List

- Adkins, L. (2010). *Coaching Agile Teams: A Companion for ScrumMasters, Agile Coaches, and Project Managers in Transition.* Addison-Wesley Professional.
- Anderson, D. J. (2010). *Kanban: Successful evolutionary change for your technology business.* Blue Hole Press.
- Ashun, P. (2021). *Agile Retrospective: Continuous Improvement and Kaizen with Scrum.* Packt Publishing.
- Beck, K., Beedle, M., Van Bennekum, A., Cockburn, A., Cunningham, W., Fowler, M., & Thomas, D. (2001). *Manifesto for Agile software development. AgileManifesto.org*
- Brown, B. (2018). *Dare to lead: Brave Work. Tough Conversations. Whole Hearts.* Random House.
- Cohn, M. (2005). *Agile estimating and planning.* Pearson Education.
- Denning, S. (2010). *The Leader's Guide to Radical Management: Reinventing the Workplace for the 21st Century.* John Wiley & Sons.
- Derby, E., & Larsen, D. (2006). *Agile Retrospectives: Making Good Teams Great.* Pragmatic Bookshelf.
- Jeffries, R. (2009). *Principles for Agile Software Development* [Image]. *Agile in a Flash.* **https://agileinaflash.blogspot.com/2009/08/12-principles-for-agile-software.htm**

- Jefferies, R. (2009). *The principles of agile software development.* XProgramming.com. https://ronjeffries.com/xprog/bookindex/
- Keith, C. (2010). *Agile Game Development with Scrum.* Pearson Education.
- Kniberg, H. (2015). *Scrum and XP from the Trenches - 2nd Edition.* Lulu.com.
- Lencioni, P. (2002). *The Five Dysfunctions of a Team: A Leadership Fable.* Jossey-Bass.
- Liker, J. K. (2004). *The Toyota way: 14 management principles from the world's greatest manufacturer.* McGraw-Hill Education.
- Medinilla, A. (2014). *Agile Kaizen: Managing Continuous Improvement far beyond retrospectives.* Springer.
- Pink, D. H. (2009). *Drive: The surprising truth about what motivates us.* Riverhead Books.
- Rubin, K. S. (2012). *Essential Scrum: A Practical Guide to the Most Popular Agile Process.* Addison-Wesley Professional
- Spotify. (2014). *Spotify Engineering Culture (Part 1).* Retrieved from **https://engineering.atspotify.com/2014/03/spotify-engineering-culture-part-1/**
- Schwaber, K., & Sutherland, J. (2017). *The Scrum Guide™: The Definitive Guide to Scrum: The Rules of the Game.* Scrum.org. Retrieved from **https://www.scrumguides.org/scrum-guide.html**
- Sutherland, J. (2014). *Scrum: The Art of Doing Twice the Work in Half the Time.* Crown Business.
- Talreja, A. (2023). *Learn Agile: Comprehensive guide to Agile principles.* https://teachingagile.com/agile
- Watts, G. (2021). *Scrum Mastery: From Good to Great Servant-Leaders*

www.ingramcontent.com/pod-product-compliance
Lightning Source LLC
Chambersburg PA
CBHW072056230526
45479CB00010B/1102